KU-615-976

STEP-by-STEP
SCIENCE

Hot and Cold

Helena Ramsay

Illustrated by Andrew Farmer
and Peter Bull

W
FRANKLIN WATTS
NEW YORK • LONDON • SYDNEY

© 1998 Franklin Watts

First published in Great Britain by
Franklin Watts
96 Leonard Street
London
EC2A 4RH

Franklin Watts Australia
14 Mars Road
Lane Cove
NSW 2006
Australia

ISBN: 0 7496 2946 0
10 9 8 7 6 5 4 3 2 1
Dewey Decimal Classification 536
A CIP catalogue record for this book is available from the British Library

Printed in Dubai

Planning and production by Discovery Books Limited
Design: Ian Winton
Consultant: Christopher Oxlade

Photographs: Action Plus: page 22 (R Francis), 30 (Glyn Kirk);
Bryan and Cherry Alexander: cover; Bruce Coleman: page 19 (Hans Reinhard);
Greg Evans: page 10, 24; Robert Harding Picture Library: page 4, 13, 25; Image Bank: page 5 bottom
(Harald Sund), 17 top (Terje Rakke); Oxford Scientific Films: page 11 (Sylvia Harcourt), 14 top
(Tom Leach), bottom (Norbert Rosing), 15 (Michael Fogden); Science Photo Library: page 9
(Jisas/Lockheed), 21 (BSIP/Cortier), 23 (Rosenfeld Images Ltd), 27 (Tek Image); Tony Stone
Worldwide: page 5 top, 7, 13 top, 17 bottom, 29 both, 30; Zefa: page 8.

ROTHERHAM LIBRARY &
INFORMATION SERVICES
J536.5
B480086991
2/02281
SCHOOLS STOCK

Contents

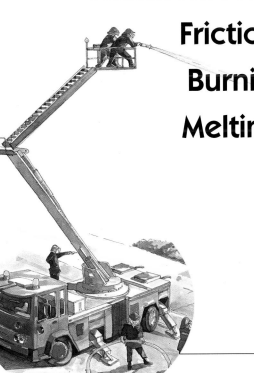

Hot and Cold

Without heat we couldn't cook our food or warm up our houses in cold weather.

On hot days we enjoy swimming in cool water, having a cold drink or eating an ice cream.

Without heat from the sun, the Earth would be a freezing, dead planet. Plants could not live and animals would have no food.

Countries close to the Equator, an imaginary line around the middle of the Earth, always have warm weather. As you travel further away from the Equator it gets colder.

4

The North and South Poles are always cold. This picture shows the South Pole. It is the coldest place in the world.

Death Valley, California, USA is one of the world's hottest places.

Temperature

Temperature tells us how hot or cold something is.

Hot things have a high temperature.

Cold things have a low temperature.

Expansion and Contraction

Everything around us is made of very tiny **particles**. These particles are always on the move. When something is heated the particles move more quickly. The more it is heated, the faster the particles move and the further away they move from one another.

Fast-moving particles take up more space than slow-moving ones. This is why things get a bit bigger when they are heated. This is called **expansion**.

At lower temperatures particles move more slowly and take up less space.

Most things get a bit smaller when they are cooled. We call this **contraction**.

6

The metal and concrete used to build bridges can expand quite a lot on hot days. Bridges have to be designed with a gap at each end to allow for expansion. The bridge rests on rollers which allow it to get longer and shorter.

Years ago, wheels for carts were made like this –

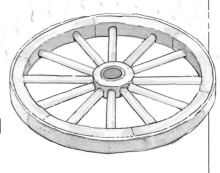

The metal rim was heated, until it expanded enough to fit over the wooden wheel.

As the metal cooled it contracted and gripped the wheel tightly.

Tram wheels are still made in this way.

Heat on the Move

Heat moves all the time. It spreads out, always travelling from hot things to cooler ones. Ice cubes make our drinks cooler because the warmth from the drink travels into the cool ice cube.

There are three ways that heat can travel – by **conduction**, by **convection** or by **radiation**.

Heat can travel through solid things like metal and wood. We call this conduction.

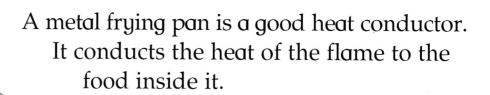

A metal frying pan is a good heat conductor. It conducts the heat of the flame to the food inside it.

The handle of the frying pan is made from wood. The handle stays cool because wood is a poor conductor.

Heat can move easily through liquids and gases by convection. It travels in moving **currents**. We call these convection currents.

Unlike convection and conduction, radiation does not need another substance to travel through. When the sun heats the Earth by radiation, its rays travel through the **vacuum** of space.

Hot Air

Heat travels through the air by convection, just as it does through water. When air is warmed it expands and becomes lighter than the air around it. Because it is lighter, warm air floats upwards. This is how hot air balloons work.

MAKE AIR EXPAND

1 Put a balloon over the end of a plastic bottle.

2 Plunge the bottle into a bowl of warm water. The water will warm the air in the bottle. The warm air will expand and inflate the balloon.

3 Now plunge the bottle into a bowl of cold water. What happens to the balloon?

On sunny days, draughts of warm air rise from the ground. These are called thermals. Glider pilots use thermals to push their gliders higher into the sky. Birds of prey use them to stay up in the air while they circle around, searching the ground for food.

Hot Weather

When the sun is shining and the weather is hot we wear thin, loose-fitting summer clothes. These clothes allow air to move around our bodies. The moving air carries the heat away from our bodies by convection.

On hot days it is always cooler in the shade. We use fans to keep us cool, too.

Tennis players often wear white clothes. White clothes are cooler to wear because the rays of heat from the sun reflect off the white cloth.

Clothes made from dark coloured cloth are not so cool. This is because dark colours absorb the sun's rays.

These houses are in Greece, where it is very hot in summer. Inside the houses it is always cool. This is because the white walls reflect the heat of the sun.

Many modern buildings have air conditioning. This keeps the rooms inside the building cool however hot it is outside.

Cold Weather

Sometimes we need to stop heat from moving. In winter we use heaters to warm the air in our homes. The warm air expands and rises upwards. A lot of this warm air could escape by convection and conduction.

We can stop heat from being wasted by putting a thick layer of material called **insulation** in the roof.

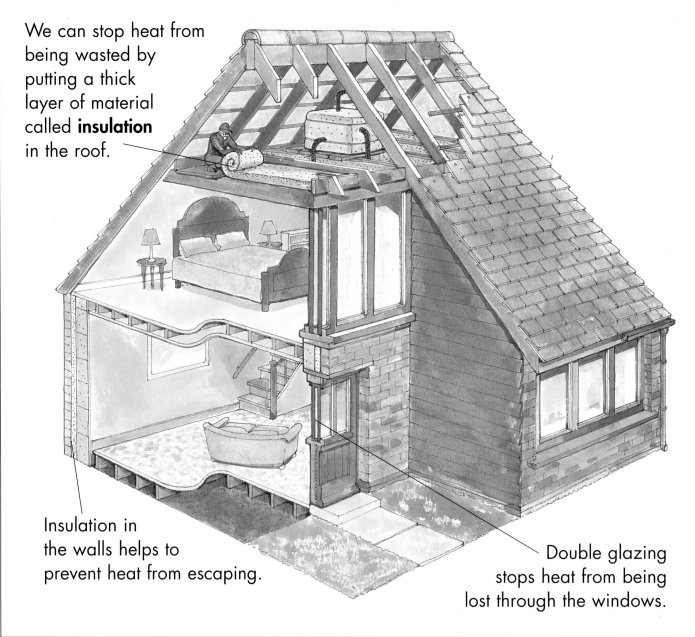

Insulation in the walls helps to prevent heat from escaping.

Double glazing stops heat from being lost through the windows.

Thick winter clothes like these are a kind of insulation. They keep us warm by trapping the air close to our bodies and stopping our body heat from being carried away by convection.

The snow on the roof of this Swiss chalet is like another layer of insulation. It helps to keep the house warm.

Beating the Weather

Many animals have to survive in places where it is very cold or very hot. In summer, the Arctic fox is a slim creature with a thin coat of grey-brown fur.

In winter the fox grows a much thicker, warmer coat which helps it to survive the Arctic cold. The fox's winter coat also acts as **camouflage** against the white snow.

Small animals, like this dormouse, often spend the coldest months of the year asleep. This is called hibernation.

In desert places many creatures spend the hottest season of the year asleep. This is called estivation. Before a snail estivates it seals up its shell with a **mucus** plug. When the mucus hardens in the heat it stops the snail from drying out.

This sand-diving lizard lives in the great heat of the Namibian desert. It can only bear the high temperature of the sand by lifting its feet off it, two at a time.

Warm Blood, Cold Blood

We are warm-blooded, like all other mammals. This means that our bodies usually stay at the same temperature. When we get too cold we shiver. Shivering makes heat in our muscles which helps to warm us up again.

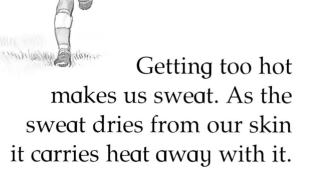

Getting too hot makes us sweat. As the sweat dries from our skin it carries heat away with it.

Reptiles like snakes, tortoises and alligators, are cold-blooded. They need the sun to keep them warm and active. When a reptile is cold it can only move slowly.

Most snakes bask in the sun after a large meal. The heat of the sun helps them to digest their food.

Panting

Did you know that dogs can't sweat? They cool down by panting. As the moisture dries from their tongues it carries the heat away with it.

Thermometers

Temperature is measured in equal units called degrees. We usually measure temperature in degrees Celsius or degrees Fahrenheit.

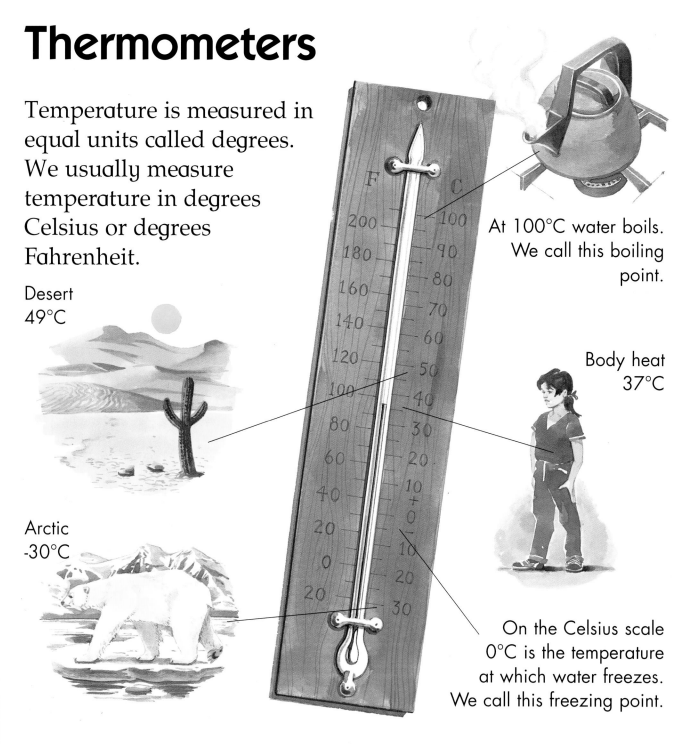

At 100°C water boils. We call this boiling point.

Desert
49°C

Body heat
37°C

Arctic
-30°C

On the Celsius scale 0°C is the temperature at which water freezes. We call this freezing point.

Most thermometers work because of expansion and contraction. The liquid inside the tube of the thermometer expands when it gets warm. This makes it reach further along the tube. When it is cold the liquid in the tube contracts.

Different kinds of thermometers are used for taking the temperatures of different things.

When we are unwell the doctor may take our temperature with a clinical thermometer.

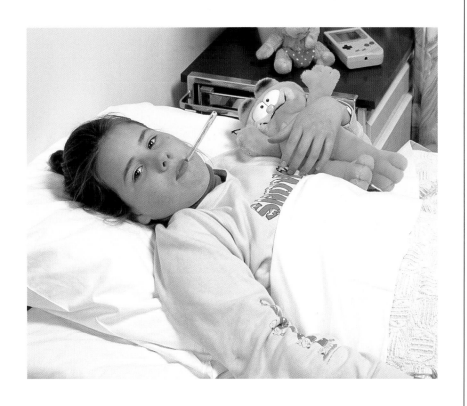

A maximum-minimum thermometer records the highest and lowest temperatures during the day and night.

Friction

We can make heat by rubbing things together. The force between two things rubbing together is called friction. The harder they are rubbed, the hotter they get. Friction can produce a lot of heat.

Wheel rim

Brake pad

Bicycle brakes use friction. The brakes rub against the rim of the wheels to slow them down. This can make the rim feel quite warm.

As a drag racing car sets off there is a loud squealing sound made by the friction of the tyres on the road.

Thousands of years ago, humans discovered that they could make fire using friction. They did it by rubbing pieces of wood together. People soon discovered that they could make meat tastier and easier to eat by heating it in the flames.

The heat produced by friction can be a nuisance. This machine drills through metal. It must be sprayed with water all the time to stop it from getting too hot.

Burning

It takes three things to start a fire – heat, air and fuel. When we heat paper or wood they burst into flames and burn into ashes.

Burning produces heat and, when there are flames, it also produces light.

While things are burning they give off smoke. Smoke is made of tiny particles of fuel that have not completely burned. A fire will continue to burn until the fuel, the air or the heat runs out.

Not all fires are started by humans. The red-hot lava flow of a volcano burns everything in its path. If a bolt of lightning strikes a tree it can begin to burn.

Melting

By adding heat we can turn solids into liquids. The particles in a solid are packed together very tightly. When it is heated its particles break away from each other and the solid melts to become a liquid.

On warm winter days the sun melts snow and ice and turns it back to water. The water fills rivers and streams.

The temperature at which a solid turns into a liquid is called its melting point. Different substances have different melting points.

These people are pouring **molten** metal into a mould. Their clothes and helmets protect them from the heat.

Boiling

When water is heated, its particles move faster and faster and its temperature rises.

In some countries, people heat water over an open fire.

When the temperature of the water reaches 100°C it stops rising, even though it is still being heated. Instead, particles of water break free and turn into gas. This is called **boiling**.

In some places, water heated by the hot rocks under the ground bursts out into the open air as a geyser.

This woman is using the hot water of the geyser to cook her food.

Freezing

Cold can turn liquids into solids. The temperature at which this happens is called freezing point. Different substances freeze at different temperatures.

Water freezes at 0°C. Frozen water is called ice. We use ice cubes to cool our drinks in summer.

On cold winter mornings everything is coated with a thin layer of ice crystals called hoar-frost.

At ice rinks water is frozen so that people can skate all-year round.

By adding salt to water we can lower its freezing point. This is why salt put onto roads and paths in winter stops them from getting dangerously icy.

MELTING ICE

1 Make some ice cubes in the freezer.

2 Take out two ice cubes and place each one on a piece of kitchen paper.

3 Sprinkle salt over one of the ice cubes.

4 Now time how long the two cubes take to melt. Which one melts fastest?

Glossary

Boiling: The point at which a heated liquid starts to turn into a gas. Boiling water turns into steam

Camouflage: Colours or markings that blend in with the background

Conduction: The way that heat travels through solid objects

Contraction: Shrinking. Things contract when they are cooled

Convection: The way that heat travels through liquids and gases

Currents: The flowing movements of heat from one place to another

Expansion: Getting bigger. Things expand when they are heated

Insulation: A layer of material that stops heat from escaping

Molten: Something that has been melted

Mucus: Slimy substance

Particles: The tiny parts of which everything is made

Radiation: The way that heat travels through empty spaces

Reflects: Makes the rays of heat from the sun bounce back

Vacuum: A completely empty space

Index